Cheryl's dry sense of humor and practical insight have helped her convey timeless messages for ... to be transformed by God's Word. True to her divinely-created and unique style, she tackles areas where spiritual growth is needed and points to the answers found in Scripture. She shares her tidbits of wisdom as a fellow struggler and offers guidance, hope, and sometimes a mild rebuke. Every day in this collection of devotional thoughts will bring encouragement and new perspective.

Debbie Tucker
Wife of Pastor Ron Tucker, Grace Church, St. Louis, MO (www.gracestl.org)

This devotional is for everyone who is ready to "grow up in every way into Christ." Cheryl has compiled a practical guide to understanding and transforming the challenges of life based on many experiences in her own life. Taking God's Word to Heart will give you deeper insight into God's character and His great love for you. The daily lessons are biblically grounded, practical, and sensitive to a wide range of situations.

Lee A. Cedra
Assoc. Pastor of Counseling, LifeLine Christian Counseling Center

Cheryl Skid's *Taking God's Word to Heart* is very practical in challenging us to apply God's Word to our everyday lives. The questions Cheryl asks are pertinent and can only be answered if the reader is honest with herself. Cheryl developed skills as a public school teacher that she now uses to teach God's people. Jesus, the Teacher, asked questions and in so doing held up a mirror, just as Cheryl does, so we can see where we are and how we look, spiritually. The Word mirror that shows us our condition is also the water that will cleanse our daily walk and get us ready for the coming of our Lord if we allow it. I have read *Taking God's Word to Heart*. Now, I must go and use the Word to remove the spots I still see on my garment. Will you join me, please?

Lilian Pickering Neede
Bible teacher and author of God's Woman Unveiled

Taking God's Word to Heart is a delightful 31-day journey where the reader can meditate on the character of God and discover implications for his or her own life. It is short and to the point, and allows the reader time to journal and meditate. It's a refreshing read for people of all ages and walks of life.

Casey Tressler
Full-time campus ministry

Cheryl Skid, with her prolific writing and studying of God's Word, has produced a wonderful new devotional: *Taking God's Word to Heart*. The book uncovers original meanings and plumbs the depths of Scripture, giving the reader greater understanding for living today. More than ever, this is a day to be rooted in the knowledge of Him, grounded in prayer, and doing the Lord's will. I recommend this devotional to set your day's course in a godly direction.

Suzanne Babarczy
Founding Director, Hearts In Action International

This book should be daily reading for women of all ages and positions in life. Each day's voyage brings the reader to a great variety of real life situations and challenges them to open their minds and hearts to God's leading. The reader is encouraged to carry a cargo of blessings for others and to be receptive of wisdom, creativity, and thoughtfulness from others. There is encouragement for the lonely or fearful. There is need to be aware and to control the trivial and thoughtless. There are reminders to listen, to be generous, to be patient, and to be full of joy and the Holy Spirit. What a great idea—the journaling pages. Every day's lesson will be just as valuable next month . . . next year. The message of the book is timeless. Everyone should own one!

Virginia Steffel
Missionary, teacher, and nurse (age 83)

Taking God's Word to Heart

31-Day Devotional Journal

CHERYL SAMELSON SKID

TAKING GOD'S WORD TO HEART

Copyright © 2011 Cheryl Samelson Skid

ISBN 978-1-886068-45-2
Library of Congress Control Number: 2011926408
Christian Life · Religious and Inspirational
Personal Growth · Faith · Self-Help

Published by Fruitbearer Publishing
P.O. Box 777, Georgetown, DE 19947 · (302) 856-6649 · FAX (302) 856-7742
www.fruitbearer.com • info@fruitbearer.com
Graphic design by Candy Abbott
Edited by Fran D. Lowe
Cover photo of St. Cyrus Nature Reserve, overlooking the North Sea, Scotland, by Cheryl Skid
Photo of author taken by Neil Skid

Printed in the United States of America

dedication

To the wonderful teachers

under whom I learned to take God's Word to heart!

table of contents

acknowledgments

I would like to recognize my mother, Mary Samelson, who taught me as early as I can remember the importance of being in community by her untiring acts of generosity and compassion.

My father, Joseph Samelson, taught me to value the least of these by his own treatment of the marginalized.

My brother, Dr. Jeffrey Samelson, is a brilliant psychologist who patiently helps me see mental health issues beneath some women's issues.

My husband, Neil, is a continual encouragement to me in my escapades, and his expertise in the kitchen draws crowds to the table.

Our daughter, Amy, has followed in my footsteps as an educator and is changing teenagers' lives!

Our daughter, Erica, is a fabulous mom, totally engaged with her two kids, who somehow finds time to pursue her passion of creating and selling beautiful desserts through her business, *The Chocolate Rooster*.

Our son, Nathan, is an award winning photographer and multi-media reporter.

Our grandchildren are the joy of our lives.

My publisher, Candy Abbott, transformed my raw material into a work of art.

introduction

A NOTE FROM CHERYL

I was raised in a Jewish home. When Jesus preciously invaded my life in 1978, I knew NOTHING about being a Christian woman! In 1983 the Lord spoke to my heart that I should teach women through the Psalms. ME! Teach women? But I did. On September 29, 1983, I taught my first lesson from the Psalms, starting with Psalm 1:1-3. Since that day I have continued to teach the Psalms, line by line, for twenty-seven years. *Taking God's Word to Heart* draws from the four hundred lessons I have written and taught women in the United States and abroad.

Taking God's Word to Heart can benefit the reader in three ways: (1) the Scripture provides the opportunity for her to judge her own behavior against God's standard; (2) the narrative for the day challenges her with practical application to use in her home or community; and (3) the journal pages offer a place to record the insight she gleans from each lesson. We often don't know what is in our hearts until we start writing. Words come forth, bringing from the depth of our hearts secrets that have been hidden even from ourselves. It's when we see the truth about ourselves that we can begin the necessary changes. You may want to use the *Taking God's Word to Heart* journaling pages right away or later to record new insights and changes that have taken place in your own heart.

I would love to hear from you! Read my blog www.cherylsvision.blogspot.com for more information and stories. You may e-mail me at cherylskid@gmail.com. I'll take your letters to heart!

"From where the sun rises to where it sets,

You inspire shouts of joy."

(Psalm 65:8 NLT)

day 1

CHANGE THE ATMOSPHERE

We walk into a room, anticipating a lovely time of fellowship, but something's wrong. It's as if we can feel a heavy grey blanket falling over us and suffocating us of any sense of pleasure. What is it about certain people who seem to drain joy out of the environment? We have all experienced it. We come home in a great mood, but whoever is on the other side of the door changes it immediately. We walk into the office hoping for a good day, yet the negative atmosphere is palpable.

Instead of letting the present atmosphere drain us, we can change it! How? Smile. Start a pleasant conversation. Offer to help. One person can make a difference. She can either light up a room or blow out the candle.

Let's let God determine our mood—not our companions, our colleagues, or our family. We can change the mood in any environment. As we set the bar for joy and peace, others will follow. Of course, some may ridicule us, but they're still watching. How many of us have been flabbergasted as that one who had scoffed at us now slinks to us in secret when her life is in shambles?

Let's check our mood. Are we the one who brings gloom, or sunshine? If we are gloomy, how can we change it? If we are sunny, how can we spread it? If we're affected by the negativity of others, how can we shield ourselves?

"Then you will call upon Me and go and pray to Me,

and I will listen to you."

(Jeremiah 29:12 NKJV)

day 2

LISTEN!

We're talking to someone about something personal that we're risking telling, and then it happens. The person to whom we're speaking breaks eye contact and scans behind us. We're left feeling insignificant. Do we do that? Are we the ones who hate being stuck in a conversation when that networking wonder might be in another part of the room? When someone calls our name, do we quickly look up as if we're thinking, *Whew! A chance to get away!*

If listening is important to God, it should be important to us! If He promises to listen to the one who comes to Him, shouldn't we listen to the one who comes to us?

I'm one whose ear can pick up bits of conversation in all directions. Maybe that comes with being a teacher. Or maybe it's an excuse. Why can't we pay attention to one person? Are we watching for terrorists, waiting for Ms. or Mr. Opportunity, or just feeling awkward standing and looking into someone's face? We can be those rare women who hold people with their eyes and leave them feeling cherished.

Maybe it isn't in your culture to look in people's eyes. How can you prove that you are listening? Who listens to you?

"But Noah found grace in the eyes of the Lord."

(Genesis 6:8 NKJV)

day 3

THE GRACE DISPENSER

How do we feel when someone overlooks a mistake we made? A flaw in our performance? A social blunder? I love grace—when it's directed toward me. But how likely am I to overlook a mistake someone else makes, particularly when it affects production or an outcome of mine? Do I cringe when a friend or family member makes a faux pas in front of someone I'm trying to impress? Yes, grace feels so good when it comes my way, but am I a grace dispenser?

Do we pride ourselves in being able to spot the typographical error? Do we feel compelled to correct someone else's child? Oh, God!! Help us to be as delighted in giving out grace to others as we are in receiving it. Grace is: no ticket on our windshield when the time on the parking meter has expired, the forgiveness of debt on a foolishly made purchase, tears of forgiveness on the face of someone we've wronged.

Help us loosen up, Lord, and not be so quick to judge. Help us love one more time, even though we've been hurt. Help us say, "It's OK" and mean it when a casserole dish is returned with a chip.

The word "grace" is found 170 times in the Bible. Lord, I love stories of extended grace, stories of people who give selflessly. Lord, let me BE one of those stories. Please work Your grace into the fabric of my life so that grace is a natural response for me.

Today, make a note of a time when you had every "right" to judge but chose to dispense grace. We can become natural grace dispensers if we do it so often that it becomes a habit.

"You hear, O Lord, the desire of the afflicted."

(Psalm 10:17 NIV)

day 4

LISTEN TO THE AFFLICTED

We long to be heard. Take a look at a child with an adult. What does she do to be heard? First, "Mom." Next, "Mom!" Then, "MOM!" If these get no results, we may see and hear the child tapping on the arm, pulling on the skirt, whining, raising the voice, rolling on the floor, losing his/her temper, or throwing objects. Wives, when not heard, may resort to nagging, pulling down the newspaper, turning off the TV, standing in front of the computer, or resorting to a resentful week of the silent treatment. Entire people groups go unheard, and their frustration can end in violence or even acts of terrorism.

Do we truly listen to each other? When a friend is talking to us, are we mentally thinking of the next thing to do? Are we wondering how much longer we have to sit here, when there are so many urgent things on our lists? Some of us never learned to listen because we were never heard. We don't know what it looks like or feels like to have someone's undivided attention. Many counselors will agree that their clients long to be heard, and actually, that is why they are there.

Why is it so hard to listen? Are we too busy? Do we think we're too important? There are those who ramble endlessly to anyone and everyone, and frankly, that's wearing. But thankfully, they are few. So, let's listen to one another. We can occasionally rephrase what a woman is saying so that she knows she was heard. The next time we see her, we can refer to that conversation as a bridge of communication, as well as to reinforce the fact that we were listening. Write about it.

"Now hope does not disappoint, because the love of God has been poured out

in our hearts by the Holy Spirit who was given to us."

(Romans 5:5 NKJV)

day 5

Drench Yourself in God's Love

There is no end to God's love for us. There is no place in our hearts that His love can't reach, no hurt in our lives that His love can't soothe, no wound in our soul so deep that God's love cannot salve. So why do we sometimes become sharp with others, avoid people, or stay away from events because we don't want to have to encounter particular individuals? Do we decline invitations, refuse to answer the phone, or choose not to respond to friendly e-mails? Do we feel lifeless, dull, and devoid of emotion?

Perhaps we need an immersion into the love of God. In the Old Testament, women would enter the Mikvah, a pool of water used for ceremonial purification. Tradition also states that a person cannot enter into a holy place until the Mikvah, or immersion. Today Orthodox women enter the Mikvah after their time of menstruation. For ten days before menstruation, the observant Jewish couple refrains from sexual intercourse; the night after Mikvah they come together as an intimate couple.

Perhaps we need an immersion—not into a ritual bath, but into a fresh revelation of God's love. At times, I have felt dry and out of sorts to the extent that I was of no use to anyone. It wasn't until I came away into a time of prolonged immersion into God's presence that those springs of rejoicing started welling up inside me again. When we are filled with the love of God, it will surely splash onto the people around us. Write about your own dryness or refreshing. What do you need?

"What man of you, having a hundred sheep,

if he loses one of them, does not leave the ninety-nine in the wilderness,

and go after the one which is lost until he finds it?"

(Luke 15:4 NKJV)

day 6

Go After the One

Do you notice the one standing alone when others are gathered in chattering groups? The child oddly dressed when others are in their little designer outfits? An elderly person shopping alone at the local market? Jesus left the ninety-nine and went after the one. What implications does that have for us?

There are groups on the look-out for those who are lonely. The gang provides a "family" to the alienated youngster. The cult promises a sense of belonging: significance. How many city youth are we losing to gangs? How many stragglers are we losing to cults? As believers, we need to imitate Jesus, who went after the one.

It's tempting to want to be among people like ourselves. It's awkward to make conversation with someone who doesn't want to talk. It is frustrating to push against walls and gates of self-protection. So why go after the one? Once you have drawn someone out of the pit, invested time and patience in her, and brought her into wholeness, giving her the courage to pursue dreams she didn't know she had, you'll know why. What a joy! Go after the one.

Sometimes I am the one. I remember being at a retreat and trying to sit down. Time after time I was told, "That seat is taken." What if I was a wounded sheep, told time after time, "That place is taken"? Well, you draw your own conclusion.

Today, let's go after the one.

"Whatever you have said in the dark will be heard in the light,

and what you have whispered behind closed doors

will be shouted from the rooftops for all to hear!"

(Luke 12:3 NLT)

day 7

THE UNPLEASANT PROMISE

"Please don't tell anyone! She told me, and I promised not to tell, but it's so awful that I had to tell someone! I feel so sorry for her!" Then one day in tears, the wounded sister approaches with the news that her secret is out.

Where do we go with the blame, the embarrassment, and the sense of betrayal? The Word has promises that are sobering as well as joyous. One such sobering promise is that words spoken in secret will be shouted from the rooftops.

The fact is this: if we want to make sure nothing gets spoken abroad, we must refrain from telling that first person. When our secret gets back to us, it is just the Word confirming itself. There is no one to blame. There is no guarantee that our secret won't be revealed, because the Word is still true, whether we speak to an acquaintance or a professional.

How can we handle such a breach of trust? Perhaps we can realize that God is more interested in our character development than the security of our reputations. Can we forgive the trust-breaker? Of course. But let's remember that ALL of God's promises, even the ones we don't like, are yes and amen!

What has been your experience? What is the Lord speaking to you?

"Search me, O God,

and know my heart: try me,

and know my thoughts."

(Psalm 139:23 KJV)

day 8

LIGHT MY DARKNESS

What is it about the dark that can be so terrifying? A pleasant room in broad sunlight can seem like a chamber of horrors when the lights are out.

Why does night play havoc with our emotions? I may feel perfectly safe during the daylight hours. But the minute I lay my head on the pillow, I am visited by swirling doubts: *Did I handle that correctly? What did she really mean when she said that? What is going to happen when he reads that e-mail tomorrow?*

What about the dark heart? The Lord wants access to every part of us. Does the Holy Spirit come in like an uninvited inspector equipped with infrared goggles? Does He bang through the doors of our hearts, trampling with His big boots?

No. If we are going to have the Holy Spirit inspect those dark places in our hearts, we must invite Him as David did in Psalm 139:23. The truth is that we don't want to face it ourselves. It takes courage to invite the Holy Spirit in to inspect our hearts because, unlike some inspectors, He won't just make a few notes and leave. He will bring those truths to our attention and expect us to face them. Once faced, we must do something to change.

Many of us never outgrow our fear of the dark: physical darkness, emotional darkness, and the dark places in the heart. It is that dark place of the heart that often sabotages our relationships. Is it worth it to face the dark places? Yes.

"To everything there is a season,

and a time to every purpose under heaven."

(Ecclesiastes 3:1 KJV)

day 9

TOO BUSY FOR FRIENDSHIPS?

Seasons of life change. When we are in school, much of our time is spent studying. When we are in school and working, we have even less free time. If we are one of the many women who are in school and working, married, and raising children, "free time" is not part of our vocabulary. Yet we still care about our friends!

Some of us suddenly reconnect with family members from whom we've been estranged. Family reconciliation takes time, and real friends will understand that. Yet friends are important, and keeping real friends takes effort!

A rewarding but often exhausting time that seems to squeeze out friendships is the caregiver season. When a loved one is under our care, we simply don't have the freedom to enjoy our friends. However, we need friends who can bolster our mental health at such critical times.

A wife raising three children, I was also working full time and attending graduate school. I'm very social. Oh, how I missed my friends! There just wasn't time! Or was there?

With a little planning and creativity, we can keep the communication lines open. Are friendships important to you? Are you spending less and less time with friends? Jot down some ways you can maintain friendships at this very busy time of life.

"She is like the merchants' ships;

she bringeth her food from afar."

(Proverbs 31:14 KJV)

day 10

SHIP OF HOPE

As a new believer hungry for more of the Word, I longed to be with people who could open the gospel to me. I took my Bible to every social function, hoping and knowing that people would open the Scriptures and I'd learn something. I'll never forget the first women's outing I went on that was held by a local church known for their godly women! I had visited their homes. They taught their children to do chores: I saw their charts on their fridges. They tended the needy: I watched them prepare casseroles for neighbors. So I was excited about the evening that was coming when I would be spending time with them. I couldn't wait to get more and more of the Word! Was I disappointed! We gathered together, and the talk was about nothing besides acquiring purchases. I heard about antiques and clothing and cars. What empty conversation!

Then the day came a few years later. A woman came to my house, and we talked about trivial things. As she left, she said, "I came to get the Word, and all I got was empty talk!"

We can consider ourselves the ships that bring food from afar. Everyone we meet during the day is standing on the port, waiting for that ship. We can come alongside and bring refreshing news of hope and gladness from the Word of God, or we can bring empty cases.

What fills our ship? How can we make sure that the cargo we carry is fresh and full of hope? Let's consider today how we can be like the ship that comes from afar, carrying good food.

"Therefore encourage one another

and build each other up,

just as in fact you are doing."

(1 Thessalonians 5:11 NIV)

day 11

ENCOURAGE SOMEONE TODAY

How do people feel when they leave our company? Do they feel built up, or torn down? Do they feel refreshed, or drained? Do they feel comforted, or condemned?

People long for encouragement, and the world gives so little! When we encourage others, we give hope and strength. When we discourage them, we may prevent them from continuing, or crush their dreams, making their progress difficult.

Some people may become so discouraged that they seem almost paralyzed. How important it is, then, to bring the encouraging word, to bring people to the place where they can hope again.

How can we encourage others? We must take our eyes and ears off ourselves and let our focus be outward. Haven't you ever been in the company of a woman you haven't seen in months or years, and she brags about her job, her husband, her children, and her home but doesn't even inquire about yours? Pretty dismal, right?

We can't do anything about how other people communicate caring, but we can do something about how we do it. Smiling, asking questions, and giving thoughtful feedback may be all the encouragement some women need to make it through the day.

How has someone encouraged you when you were at your lowest? What effect did it have on you? Take a look around. Some women who seem distant and uninterested may just have lost hope to reach out. Be the encouragement someone needs today.

"And the disciples were continually

filled with joy and with the Holy Spirit."

(Acts 13:52 NASB)

day 12

STAY FRESH!

We are in the midst of an international conference, and enthusiasm is high. Worship starts and swells, making spirits soar. The speakers lead us through a variety of emotions. After the last meeting, hearts are full—new friends are made and old ones made closer. Jesus is so real and so close!

Then comes the time to go home. How do those words make you feel? You may have a great family life, so you are excited about sharing what you learned when you walk through the door. Or like many women, you may have a difficult home life, so you dread the reactions that await your return. What if the excitement of the last three days is sucked into a vacuum of sarcasm? Can we retain the joy that we received during those meetings?

Our Scripture today tells us that the disciples were continually filled with joy and the Holy Spirit. The same Spirit that was in them abides in us. We can welcome His Spirit now. We can learn to be intimate with Jesus in any situation. The disciples faced difficult circumstances daily! They were regularly mocked and challenged, yet they were full of joy and the Holy Spirit.

Circumstances change. People may or may not share our enthusiasm. But there is One who is constant and never changes. That One lives in us and is always ready for a feast! How about writing Him a letter right now?!

"For I am confident of this very thing,

that He who began a good work in you

will perfect it until the day of Christ Jesus."

(Philippians 1:6 NASB)

day 13

GROWING PAINS

You are born again. The chief cornerstone is laid. The building that is your life will never be shaken! Right? WRONG! Just because Jesus is Lord of our lives and we have made a commitment to follow Him does not guarantee that things will go smoothly. Once we have accepted Christ and made a genuine decision to put Him first in our lives, it is often the beginning, not the end, of turmoil.

Consider this as an example. You have looked at the crooked mess that is your mouth and realize that you need an orthodontist. You know that your mouth would be more beautiful and delightful as a result of orthodontic work. You carefully choose an orthodontist, make a phone call, and set up an appointment. On your first appointment you even pay in full. Is your mouth gorgeous now? No! Why not? You made a decision! You were sincere! You even paid for it.

We know that there is a lot of work between the heartfelt decision to undergo orthodontia and the end result. Why? Much has to be done! There are things that have to be moved, causing great pain. In dire situations, some cutting away may even be required. Weekly visits allow us to see how far we've come, but they also remind us of how far we have to go.

That's a simple illustration to show us how important it is to realize that even though the Christian walk is a process involving pain and removal, it is so worth the end result. Our Great Orthodontist who began the work will also see that it is completed beautifully. What changes have you seen so far?

"My soul shall make [her] boast in the Lord;

the humble shall hear of it and be glad."

(Psalm 34:2 NKJV)

day 14

REJOICE IN OUR BLESSINGS—BOAST IN THE LORD

We use the word "pride" casually. We take pride in our baseball team. We're proud of our children's report cards. We're proud when we finally graduate, buy the first car, or move into a house. But the word PRIDE in the Bible carries a meaning that implies majesty, exaltation, and honor—attributes that only belong to God.

We find that human pride has weak legs; it can't stand up under the pressure of failure. If we are proud of our accomplishments and they fail, our legs crumble under us. If we are proud of our children's academic record, but then they fall into drugs and drop out of school, our legs fold. If we are proud of the perfect marriage, but the spouse wanders, our legs turn to water.

So how can we genuinely be happy about blessings without carrying pride around like a trophy? Is there a kind of boasting that does not run people off, make them depressed, or cause them to cringe? Yes. When we boast in the Lord, we gladden people's hearts because everyone who loves Jesus has equal access to Him, His goodness, and provision. So let's boast of Jesus' beautiful attributes. They are within the reach of all who love Him.

Write about your blessings and the One who gave them to you. Begin thanking Him for the blessings of other people, realizing that it is foolish to be jealous when He has chosen to bless another! Appreciate what God has given you, and you'll see the joy that starts to fill your heart. When we truly know that ALL GOOD THINGS come from God, all our boasting will be in the Lord.

"Take therefore the talent from him,

and give it unto him which hath ten talents."

(Matthew 25:28 KJV)

day 15

APPRECIATE AND USE YOUR TALENTS

As we discussed yesterday, we are not to boast in ourselves, yet God does tell us to use our talents. If God gave us talents, then we are ungrateful and disrespectful to God when we leave them unused in the drawer, stuffed in a pocket, hidden under the bed, or locked in a box.

Not all of us were encouraged in our aptitudes or talents as children and thus may be timid about stepping out. But, think! What just comes "naturally" to you? Do you find yourself organizing things? Are you a good listener? Is it easy for you to give advice for which people are grateful? Do others often compliment you on your grooming or wardrobe? Do you find yourself studying continually? Do you look for reasons to take meals to people? Does it give you pleasure to give people rides? Do you round up children to teach? Do you make friends easily? Do people continually ask you for recipes? Do you love building things? Do you create beauty around you? Do you have an aptitude for technology? Are you the one everyone asks to assemble that tricky Christmas present?

God has placed talents within you to use so they'll multiply. What might start out as a little hobby or favor can grow into a huge business. Your small group of five people meeting in your living room may increase to the point that it will fill a stadium. Timidity, which prevents us from using our talents, does not please the Lord!

Start thinking about what you LOVE doing, and spend more time doing those things. Read up on how you can do them better. Find someone else who excels in that area and ask her questions. Journal through the next thirty days, and you may be surprised what you notice.

"So the Lord spoke to Moses face to face,

as a man speaks to his friend."

(Exodus 33:11 NKJV)

day 16

BEST FRIENDS

I love thinking about how I first met each close friend of mine. I met Joanne in third grade. Brand new to the school, I was told to sit in a huge desk so big that my feet hung stiffly in front of me. Joanne came up to me and said, "I'll be your friend." And she was. She still is, all of these past forty-five years.

I met Kathleen like this: I was a distributor in direct sales. After going through the list of all my friends, I was at the end of my contacts. I decided to open the big, fat St. Louis phone book and pick a name at random. I called the name. The stranger said sure, I could come over and show her my products. She became one of my best friends, and we're still very close friends thirty-one years later.

De was standing in front of me in a long bathroom line at a local venue where the Imperials were going to perform. After introducing myself, I found out that we went to the same church and lived in the same suburb. We became wonderful friends and have been for thirty years.

Do friends matter to God? Oh yes! Relationships matter very much to God. Jesus' disciples were His friends. Mary and Martha were His friends. We are His friends. When did you meet this best Friend you will ever have? If He really is a friend, you don't meet Him one day and forget Him but then say He has been a friend for thirty years. Friendship has to be cultivated.

Think about five of your friends. How have they enriched your life? And how about Jesus? Start writing!

"But the fruit of the Spirit is love,

joy, peace, longsuffering, gentleness, goodness, faith,

meekness, temperance: against such there is no law."

(Galatians 5:22-23 KJV)

day 17

DEVELOP A TASTE FOR FRUIT

Sometimes I throw away my common sense about food and start to binge on things like chips, cake, and cookies—all those foods that add pounds, inches, and disease but no benefits. During those times I don't LOVE fruit. But when I'm eating right and have purged "junk" out of my diet, fruit is DELIGHTFUL. Fruit is DELICIOUS and REFRESHING. Junk food deadens my desire for fruit.

Maybe it is that way in our spiritual walk. We may give ourselves over to coarse jesting, gossiping, and idle talk. We may start watching movies and television shows that don't glorify God but instead draw us into sinful thinking. During that time we may lose our taste for spiritual things. When that happens, we need to create in ourselves a hunger for the things of God. It may require cleansing and purging our hearts by radically changing what we see and hear.

Take your own spiritual pulse. Are you longing to spend time with people who exude love, joy, peace, patience, kindness, goodness, meekness, gentleness, and self-control? Or are you looking for a carnal good time? Are you drawn to those whose hearts are at peace, or the one who can tell you where the party is? We can have fun and still live a fruit-filled life. In the days to come, we are going to spend some time learning and writing about the fruit of the Spirit.

How good does fruit look to you right now?

"We love Him

because He first loved us."

(1 John 4:19 NKJV)

day 18

LOVE: A FRUIT OF THE SPIRIT

Good deeds! Can they be checked off the list like "clean the garage"? Is there a reason to keep "track" of how much kindness we are distributing? In 1989 President George H.W. Bush gave his inaugural address, challenging each citizen to be one of a thousand points of light in making a change for good in the lives of others. Floods, hurricanes, and earthquakes have devastated communities, prompting groups to help and give. The 2000 movie, *Pay It Forward*, showcases people doing random acts of generosity after being recipients of generous acts.

From where does the desire to do good originate? Are we born wanting to be kind or generous? Watch a two-year-old. Is he joyful about sharing his favorite toys? Is she happy when an intruder plops on Mommy's lap? Children seem to be born selfish until they are taught that there is a better way. The Bible teaches us not to return evil for evil, but to return good for evil. It doesn't come naturally to us. We have our feelings hurt in elementary school, and we come home crying. Someone steals our handbag, and we want retribution. A company makes an enormous error of judgment and ruins an entire coastline, so we demand payment.

So think about it. How do people becoming loving and generous? What about you? Are you growing in love and generosity in your life? Love is a fruit of the Spirit. Write about that. Today, what is your love capacity? Your generosity quotient?

"But let all those that put their trust in thee rejoice:

let them ever shout for joy;

because thou defendest them:

let them also that love thy name be joyful in thee."

(Psalm 5:11 KJV)

day 19

JOY: A FRUIT OF THE SPIRIT

According to the manual that came with the gift my husband gave me for my birthday, the Palm Pilot can do all kinds of amazing things. But mine does only the one basic operation because, whether due to my laziness, apathy, casual approach, low frustration level, or impatience, I don't enjoy this marvel of technology. Consider salvation. Salvation comes with loaded benefits. It takes study, persistence, determination, and patience to gain the understanding to appropriate even a small percentage of the benefits that are part of the salvation "package." Unlike my gadget, which may require upgrading or even replacement because of obsolescence, salvation is fresh, complete, and always the latest model.

A fruit is defined in part as something harvested by humans. Some time ago, I was living in Israel on a kibbutz during harvest season. We were each told that in addition to our normal tasks, we were supposed to add harvest to our day. We were ordered to report to the fields and put in focused hard work so that the crops would be gathered.

JOY is a benefit of salvation and a fruit of the Spirit. If the Holy Spirit has residence in our hearts, then we have joy—His joy. His joy is steady. It doesn't come in spurts. Joy is available because it is part of the package of salvation. The fruit of joy doesn't come from our surroundings. The Holy Spirit and His joy trumps everything that happens around us. Let's do all it takes to tap into His many benefits of salvation and enjoy the fruit.

"For ye have need of patience,

that, after ye have done the will of God,

ye might receive the promise."

(Hebrews 10:36 KJV)

day 20

PATIENCE: A FRUIT OF THE SPIRIT

It seemed to me that my daughter moved in slow motion. Getting her into her clothes, into the car seat, and out of the car seat seemed to take minutes longer than necessary. I would tap my foot, roll my eyes, and think, "Come on! We need to get going!" Then one day I decided to watch her. I stopped concentrating on what I was doing and where I was going, and just let my eyes remain on her. I watched as her mind seemed to slowly and methodically send messages to her little arms and legs. She was just waiting for the signals to reach her limbs.

Sometimes when we are waiting to see God move, we forget that we are not the only players in this game of kingdom life. There are other minds to reach, hearts to touch, and plans to change before that for which we are believing can become that which we can see!

Some of us in the Western world are ruled by our watches, date books, and schedules. Many of us seem to have internalized those timepieces, actually feeling our hearts racing as time approaches for this or that and pieces just aren't falling into place. God does not operate within time as we know it. Instead, He moves and woos hearts, one at a time. Like my daughter, players in our world each sense time differently.

We can't lose patience with people, or we will do more harm than good. Instead of being able to hear and respond to God, they're hearing and responding to our subtle or blunt irritation. Can we trust God? Yes, because at the right time, He brought us to Himself!

"She opens her mouth with wisdom,

and on her tongue is the law of kindness."

(Proverbs 31:26 NKJV)

day 21

KINDNESS: A FRUIT OF THE SPIRIT

T.H.I.N.K. My friend's post on Facebook asked, "Do you **think** before you speak? Are your words True? Helpful? Inspiring? Necessary? Kind?" I thought about that. Separately, each of those qualities of communication can hurt—except one. True words can hurt: "I saw your husband last night kissing another woman in a parked car." Helpful words can hurt: "I can help you find a dress that doesn't make you look so frumpy." Inspiring words can hurt: "Your children's stepmother is amazing! Those children have never been so well-behaved, successful in school, or happy. What an inspiration that woman is to all stepmothers!" Necessary words can hurt: "Unless you do something about your breath, you will lose friends." But kindness? Kindness never hurts.

Kindness is the sheep's wool in the slipper of the ballerina, keeping the toes safe from the jarring caused by contact with the floor. It's the amniotic fluid around the baby, keeping him safe when Mom makes sudden moves. It's the strong arms of a husband around his wife when they look down at their child on a gurney being taken into surgery. It's the safe porch in a storm, where the danger can be seen and not felt.

Kindness NEVER hurts. Kindness wraps, shelters, protects, and shields. Lord! Above all, help my words be kind. When I speak true, helpful, inspiring, necessary words, please remind me to wrap them in kindness.

How about you? How can you wrap your true, helpful, inspiring, necessary words in kindness? Write about your kindness journey.

"Whatever good the Lord will do to us,

the same we will do to you."

(Numbers 10:32 NKJV)

day 22

GOODNESS: A FRUIT OF THE SPIRIT

Difficulties will come. Our reaction to them makes the difference between flourishing fruit and stunted fruit. We CAN embrace difficulties. As we embrace the difficulties in our lives, we fertilize the fruit of goodness.

It's easy to love the cute baby, the sweet friend, or the kind elderly gentleman. But the troublemaker at work? The cynic in the family? The neighbor who calls the city every time she sees a weed growing in our yard? Embracing those unlovely ones fertilizes our goodness fruit.

Goodness does the right thing always, even if someone isn't watching. Goodness is the heart that hides no evil secrets. Goodness is the open hand that doesn't clutch in greed or selfishness. Suppose we're financially pinched, and we notice some money lying out in the lunch room. Choosing to be honest when faced with something that could be a quick fix is a goodness fertilizer. Perhaps we are selling a car. We'd get much more money for it if it hadn't been in an accident. But it has! A big one. Choosing to disclose what could hurt us financially is applying the goodness fertilizer. Maybe we're scheduled to work in the church nursery when we're suddenly invited to a friend's barbecue. We could say that we are sick. Choosing to fulfill our obligation when it's inconvenient is a goodness fertilizer. Let's take an inventory today of all those fertilizing moments we didn't recognize before. How will this knowledge help us face hardships in the future?

"He that is faithful in that which is least

is faithful also in much."

(Luke 16:10a KJV)

day 23

FAITHFULNESS: A FRUIT OF THE SPIRIT

About the faithful: We know they'll be on time. We know that their part of the project will be done well. We know that their word is enough. Faithfulness is a fruit of the Spirit, and as such, is resident within us when we are born again.

Years ago I used to make excuses. If I made plans with someone but something better came up, I would find a way to get out of the obligation. I used to take sick days if I wasn't really sick but just wanted to stay home. I would justify it by saying to myself, "Well, I stay late and come in early—so what's the difference if I take this day off?" I used to sign up to attend workshops, but then cancel. Why do we shun faithfulness? Are we afraid of being controlled?

We need to look at what faithfulness really is. If a person is faithful, she supports others. She's established, so she has a track record. Her words are matched by her actions. She won't cave in under pressure or run off when the going gets rough. The faithful woman is the one we can trust to be our birthing coach if our husband isn't home, take care of the pets when we're out of town, or tend our newborns.

Are you faithful? Can people count on you? What are the areas in which you are not faithful? Remember, if it is a fruit of the Spirit, it must be tended. Try growing your faithfulness muscles by sticking to your word, finishing that unpleasant task, or refusing to quit. Write about it.

"That He would grant you,

according to the riches of his glory,

to be strengthened with might by his Spirit in the inner man."

(Ephesians 3:16 KJV)

day 24

SELF-CONTROL: A FRUIT OF THE SPIRIT

Some researchers are concluding that self-control is exhaustible. They are finding that we have a finite amount of self-control; exerting it is painful, and eventually it will give out. Like a flimsy cover preventing water from gushing into a hole in a boat, our self-control will finally give way and the undesirable will come rushing in. That would explain why we have EVERY INTENTION of getting off the computer . . . but by the time we look at the clock, three hours have passed. Or we make every effort to stay away from the cookie aisle, deliberately shopping on only the outer perimeter of the grocery store where the fresh fruits, veggies, meats, and dairy products are located. But then, *zooooom*! Our grocery cart heads STRAIGHT for the refined carbs, and we leave laden with everything we said we wouldn't touch!

That is SELF-control. What about the fruit of self-control? How does that differ from the control we painfully, with gritted teeth, exert before the cave-in? If self-control is a fruit of the Spirit of Christ that dwells in us, we have to believe that it is not of ourselves. Unlike our puny self-control, which, like holding our breath can only last so long until we gasp, the self-control from and by the Holy Spirit would be, like Himself, inexhaustible. Surely we can pray like Paul, that according to the RICHES OF HIS glory—not of our feebleness—He would strengthen us through HIS SPIRIT, not our self-help manual. Do you feel like caving in? Pray!

"Raise a song and strike the timbrel,

the pleasant harp with the lute."

(Psalm 81:2 NKJV)

day 25

GATES OF THE BODY: THE EARS

We have been learning about the working of the Holy Spirit within us, but we also must be aware of things we can do to protect our walk with the Lord. Are we aware of sounds around us? Right now I can hear chimes of music coming from my prayer room, along with the click of toenails as our Great Pyrenees saunters down the wood floor, the *whffff* as he slides onto his stomach, and the clunk as the chain links of his collar hit the floor.

What we hear can affect changes in our brain. In undergraduate school I noticed that when I studied while listening to Baroque music, I seemed to stay attentive to my studies with much more ease than without it. Dr. John Diamond, an Australian physician and psychiatrist, reports that the beat, noise level, and shrill sounds of rock music destroy the symmetry between the hemispheres of the brain, causing alarm to the body and lessened work effectiveness.

Maybe you have noticed that sound affects you. Consider soundtracks of movies, background music in restaurants, and ring tones! We're surrounded by music that is making a statement. What statement do we want to send our bodies?

Of course, we can't always control what we hear, but many times we can! Why not put into our ear gates those sounds that will make us more, not less effective? Write about the music you choose and why you choose it.

"Your eye is a lamp that provides light for your body.

When your eye is good, your whole body is filled with light.

But when your eye is bad, your whole body is filled with darkness."

(Matthew 6:22-23a NLT)

day 26

GATES OF THE BODY: THE EYES

We can protect our walk with the Lord by what we allow in front of our eyes. What a miracle is sight! Small oval organs in the face bring in a world. When our daughters were two and four and a half years old, I left them watching a children's program on TV while I went into the adjacent kitchen to start lunch. I walked back into the room and saw them watching a human birth broadcast live! My daughters had been looking intently in one direction, but the content before them changed just that fast! They were not responsible for what they were watching—I was, as their mother and guardian. Although the miracle of birth is a wonder to behold, I was unaware of the change in the program, and wouldn't have casually placed it before them without any explanation.

How much attention do we pay to what is before our eyes? Gazing at a peaceful scene sends messages of peace to my brain, and thus to my entire body. Being forced to watch an act of violence, which sadly happens in many war-torn parts of the world, sends messages of anxiety and unrest to the brain as well as to the other parts of the body. Seeing acts of violence, even when we know they are simulated, sends blood flowing to the brain, inducing feelings of aggression.

How can we take control over what those for whom we are responsible see? Let's give our brains and bodies a vacation and gaze on that which is beautiful and peaceful!

"My beloved spoke, and said unto me,

'Rise up, my love, my fair one,

and come away.'"

(Song of Solomon 2:10 NKJV)

day 27

"COME AWAY!"

Do we know when it is time to come away—to lay down the daily tasks, the rushing, the responsibilities, the planning, the goal-setting, and the achieving? This Scripture gives us the answer. We know it is time to come away when we hear the sweet sound of our lover calling to us, "Come! Come away!"

Jesus wants time with us alone. He is the bridegroom wooing the bride. He is the shepherd inspecting the sheep for wounds and cuts. He is the vinedresser caressing our branches, looking for dead ones to trim away. What bride and bridegroom can have intimacy in the midst of a desperate rush to accomplish life's goals? What shepherd can inspect the skin of the sheep that is racing away from him? What tree would dare slap at the hand of the gardener?

What benefit is there in coming away? Coming away alone brings refreshing, a new perspective, an ability to go on, and new strength. Coming away with one's beloved brings new intimacy, understanding, and secrets only those two can share.

Consider your spiritual journey. Have you come away? Do you hear the voice of the bridegroom? Are you willing to *stop!* and come away to spend time alone with the Sweetest One of all? This week, pay attention to the voice of the One who loves you, as He bids you to come. Yield to it.

"He makes peace in your borders,

and fills it with the finest wheat."

(Psalm 147:14 NKJV)

day 28

BOUNDARIES: A BIBLICAL PRINCIPLE

In the first chapter of the Bible, God divided and made boundaries. He divided the heavens from the earth, light from darkness, and waters under the sky from the waters above the sky. We, too, have borders. We each have bodies that are separate and individual. Our brains contain our own thoughts, our bodies our own blood, and our hearts our own secrets.

How are we meant to function in our families, churches, communities, and workplaces as separate individuals, yet respecting others?

Today, think about this: Where do you leave off and the persons closest to you begin? Do you give others the right to their own opinions, ways to do things, and goals? Do you feel the need to impose your way of thinking on them? How about your freedom? Do you feel free to think and behave as you believe appropriate? Is someone else continually imposing his or her thoughts on you, demanding behavior that doesn't feel like "you"?

If we are functioning within our "borders," there will be peace. If we invade others' borders or others invade ours, there will be misunderstanding, discord, and strife. Today, assess the peace in your home, office, church, and community. Is there peace within your borders?

"For God is not the author of confusion

but of peace."

(1 Corinthians 14:33 NKJV)

day 29

BOUNDARIES: PEACE

Peace is mentioned over 420 times in the Bible, and Jesus is even called the Prince of Peace. If peace is so important, we must guard it. How is anything guarded? If we have an expensive treasure, don't we put it in a secure place where people can't steal it? How about our precious children? Don't we guard them with careful watching and admonitions and rules? Just as we guard objects of value and people of value, so we also need to guard our peace within our hearts. How? How do we guard anything? We consider the threats. What is the likelihood that my expensive automobile would be stolen if I leave the keys in it and the door open? What is the possibility of my child being snatched if I go to the mall and sit down to talk with a friend, letting the child wander off alone?

What can steal our peace? What we listen to and see has the capacity to steal our peace. Those gates are crucial to our peace! Certain people steal our peace. Unless we are trained counselors, listening to complaining and whining day after day from those who are idle and choose not to change their circumstances can steal our peace. Unexpected crises can suddenly steal our peace.

How do we guard our peace? Watch what we read and hear. Keep acquaintances at bay by limiting their phone calls to five minutes. Build up a reservoir of peace in our hearts so that when crises suddenly strike, we can know that the truths of the Scriptures will take us through. We can lean on the promise in Isaiah 26:3 which says that God will keep us in perfect peace if we keep our mind stayed on Him.

"So teach us to number our days,

that we may apply our hearts unto wisdom."

(Psalm 90:12 KJV)

day 30

BOUNDARIES: TIME

A few weeks ago I asked someone, "What are you doing?" The answer surprised me. "I'm wasting time." I can't imagine anyone purposely wasting time. Yet, how much of our time is, indeed, wasted? The busier we are in ministry, the more opportunities we have to see our time stolen by people who want to talk.

We have choices when that occurs. We can 1) drop everything and talk (usually listen) to that person because "this is a ministry opportunity and I need to take it"; 2) ignore the phone call or tell someone to say we're not available; or 3) plan by setting up blocks of time when we're available to listen or chat.

Most of us are discerning enough to know when someone needs immediate help, and humble enough to realize that there are plenty of other people who can effectively minister to that person. We can plan in advance how to handle interruptions so that we can guard our time.

A life without boundaries is like a city without walls. In Bible times walls were built to keep out enemies. Today there are plenty of enemies who would steal our peace regarding our time. Once we have taken a stand that time with God is essential, intruders will attempt to climb over the walls, slide through the cracks, or burrow beneath a weak foundation. We have a responsibility to create and maintain our borders.

We know we are not fighting against people, but against spiritual enemies. How can you guard your time?

"He must increase,

but I must decrease."

(John 3:30 KJV)

day 31

MORE OF YOU AND LESS OF ME

We have come to the end of our *Taking God's Word to Heart* study and journal. Hpefully we will read it again and again to continue to make necessary adjustments so that we are continually changing. Like John, our lifetime goal should be less of "me" and more of "Him."

How can there be less of me? How can there be more of His light visible to others? How can I make sure I'm not smudging the glass of the lamp that holds the oil?

As we have learned in our study together, many times we have to concentrate less on DOING and more on BEING. We may think we're spending time with God, but are we really just writing, reading, or talking? How about the quiet of sitting in His presence, doing NOTHING but breathing Him in and letting Him be who He wants to be in us at that moment?

Jesus! Jesus! Jesus! I must DECREASE in activity, in striving, in working, in pushing, in clamoring. I must rest so that You can fill those places in me that are empty and dry. Jesus! Jesus! Jesus! You are already all that You will be. But oh, how we long that more of You may be seen in us!

Today, how about setting aside time to just sit in His presence and let Him fill those places that are yet untouched by His hand? As we decrease in our desire to "do," we can be satisfied to let the precious God of Israel fulfill those ancient words: "I AM who I AM."

meet the author

Cheryl Samelson Skid was born into a Jewish family, lived for a year in Israel during the time of the Six Day War, and never had the slightest interest in Jesus or Christianity. However, in 1978, when Cheryl was on her way to report a teacher who was evangelizing in a public school, Jesus Christ came and sat in the passenger seat of her car and said, "I Am Who they say I Am. I Am the Son of God." With tears of repentance and total commitment to her newfound Savior, Cheryl entered a path that birthed *Women with a Vision* in 1983. Through this non-profit ministry, she teaches women how to grow in Christ and impact their world.

women with a vision

Cheryl graduated from Indiana University with a BA in English and from the University of Missouri– St. Louis with a masters' degree in special education. She retired after twenty-five years of teaching hundreds of students, all of whom she holds in her heart.

Although Cheryl enjoys traveling throughout the world with *Women with a Vision,* she is devoting time to writing. This is her first book.

Cheryl and Neil have been married 38 years and live in Florissant, Missouri.

order info.

For autographed copies

or to schedule speaking engagements, contact:

Cheryl Skid

Women with a Vision

P.O. Box 693

Florissant, MO 63032 USA

(314) 603-5687

cherylskid@gmail.com

$15.00 plus $6 S/H

Fruitbearer Publishing, LLC

P. O. Box 777, Georgetown, DE 19947

(302) 856-6649 • FAX (302) 856-7742

info@fruitbearer.com

www.fruitbearer.com

Made in the USA
Charleston, SC
16 April 2011